Halloween

BETTY KIRKPATRICK

Crombie Jardine
PUBLISHING LIMITED

Unit 17, 196 Rose Street, Edinburgh EH2 4AT
www.crombiejardine.com

Published by Crombie Jardine Publishing Limited
First edition, 2005

Copyright © 2005,
Crombie Jardine Publishing Limited

All rights are reserved. No part of this publication may be
reproduced, stored in a retrieval system, or transmitted,
in any form or by any means, electronic, mechanical,
photocopying, recording or otherwise, without the prior
written permission of the publisher.

ISBN 1-905102-32-1

Designed by www.glensaville.com
Printed & bound in the United Kingdom by
William Clowes Ltd, Beccles, Suffolk

CONTENTS PAGE

Introduction p.4

Haggis p.8

Halloween p.21

Hogmanay p.48

Appendix p.72

Other Scottish festivals p.101

Introduction

Scotland has many attractions. That is why so many people visit it from across the world. Of course, its most obvious attraction is the beauty of its scenery. The heather-clad peaks, the picturesque glens and the wealth of rivers and lochs together make up a landscape that is unforgettable.

True, the weather can be a problem because it is totally unpredictable. However, one of the impressive features of Scotland is that it looks beautiful in any weather. When it is grey and stormy or cloudy and snowy the Scottish landscape is just as attractive as it is when the skies are blue and the sun is shining. Indeed, some people prefer the more sombre landscapes as it means the scourge of the Highlands, the vicious biting midge, will stay away.

Scotland has much more than just its appearance to commend it. It is a country that is steeped in history, culture, legend and customs. Visible remains of its history and culture can be seen in its castles and domestic architecture and in the paintings and literature of its artists and writers.

Many of its customs live on and can be enjoyed by visitors to the country as, indeed, they are by the native inhabitants. This book looks at some of the most important of these: Scotland's national dish, haggis, and the occasion that most celebrates it (Burns' supper), Halloween and Hogmanay.

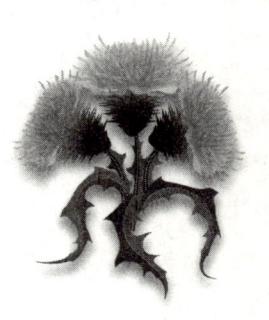

HAGGIS

Although Scotland is not generally noted for its haute cuisine it is definitely noted for its produce. For example, Scotland's Aberdeen Angus beef is known the world over, as is its smoked salmon and venison.

Discerning visitors to Scotland are likely to know about these delicacies in advance, but they may well be consumed with curiosity about what is popularly known as Scotland's national dish, haggis. Thanks to export expertise, Scots beef, salmon and venison are quite likely to have been consumed in a restaurant in the discerning visitor's own country, but haggis, well that's quite another story! We tend to keep haggis to ourselves, although there is now a flourishing export trade in haggis, mostly to ex-pat Scots in various parts of the world.

The Scots always think of haggis as being a dish that belongs exclusively to them. This was not always the case. Until the eighteenth century haggis was also eaten in England. Why the English gave up haggis is not known, but doing so was certainly their loss.

The Mystery of the Haggis

A certain mystery surrounds haggis and this mystery is one that is deliberately fostered by some Scots who tend to tease tourists about the nature of haggis. They try to get the gullible visitor to believe that the haggis is some kind of animal or bird that has to be caught before being cooked and consumed. There is even a myth that the haggis has one leg shorter than the other. This is completely untrue. The haggis has no legs at all, being neither animal nor bird.

The Truth About Haggis

It is as well for visitors to Scotland not to know the true nature of haggis before tasting it.

Haggis is absolutely delicious and most of the visitors to Scotland who are privileged to taste it enjoy it. However, some visitors never get round to tasting haggis at all, being put off by a description of how it is made. It is undeniably true that the haggis does not sound enticing, but the proof of the pudding is in the eating.

The haggis is traditionally made from a sheep's stomach that is stuffed with the offal of the sheep, the heart, lungs and liver, together with suet, oatmeal and seasoning. Several Scottish butchers sell haggis that they have made themselves to their own particular recipe. They all taste slightly different and so there is obviously a secret ingredient.

It is now possible to obtain a vegetarian version of haggis. This, of course, is not encased in a sheep's stomach and indeed the casings of some meat versions are now also man-made. The vegetarian version obviously also lacks the sheep's offal, but is, nevertheless, quite tasty.

Eating Haggis

Haggis is readily obtainable from most butchers and supermarkets and it is regularly eaten in Scottish homes where there is someone who can be bothered to cook. Traditionally eaten with mashed potato and turnips, haggis is tasty, nutritious, easy to cook and good value for money.

Those who feel like eating haggis but prefer fast food to cooking can make their way to a chip shop and purchase a haggis supper. The haggis is cooked in batter and served with chips. It is tasty enough but – be warned! – it is not nearly as good as haggis served more traditionally.

Haggis sometimes goes upmarket and is occasionally to be found on the menus of some gourmet tourist restaurants without its usual companions – mashed potatoes and turnips. Instead, it receives a more haute cuisine treatment, such as being encased in filo pastry and served with a raspberry coulis - a far cry from the traditional haggis supper!

A Burns' Supper

More Scots eat haggis on or around the anniversary of the birth of Robert Burns, January 25th, than on any other day of the year. The anniversary is celebrated by an occasion known as a Burns' supper and so many of these are held throughout Scotland that they cannot possibly all take place on the actual day. The

Burns' supper season, therefore, often extends for quite a few weeks – and a great deal of haggis is consumed.

The traditional Burns' supper is a ceremonial occasion and a large haggis is the centrepiece. The chef carries the haggis into the dining room on a silver salver and a tartan-clad piper playing the bagpipes precedes him. Homage is paid to the haggis by one of the guests who stands before it and recites a poem entitled *To a Haggis* by Robert Burns. In the poem Burns pays tribute to the virtues of the haggis and emphasises its superiority over foreign dishes. The person addressing the haggis also cuts it open at the appropriate part of the poem. *See* **Appendix**.

The haggis is served to the guests with the traditional accompaniment of mashed potatoes and turnips, known in Scots as chappit tatties and bashit neeps. Of course whisky, Scotland's national drink, is consumed in large quantities, although wine is also usually served. Some people pour whisky over the haggis before eating it.

In the course of the evening various speeches and toasts are given, principally a speech called *The Immortal Memory*, that pay tribute to the genius of Robert Burns. There is also a toast, accompanied by a short speech in some way relating to women, entitled *To the Lasses* in memory of Burns' affection and passion for the female sex. Fortunately, women have the right to reply to the toast and so they can have the last word in this exchange.

The evening also includes various songs and poems drawn from the works of Robert Burns and ends with a hearty rendition of *Auld Lang Syne* (*see* **Appendix**).

HALLOWEEN

Halloween is celebrated on October 31st. It has long been an important festival in Scotland, and is a particularly popular one with the children because they benefit most from some of the customs.

History

In the old Celtic calendar, October 31st marked both the end of summer and the end of the Celtic year and this night had supernatural associations. It was believed that the souls of the dead would revisit their old homes on that night and that evil spirits would roam the land, making it a night for sensible people to stay indoors. While they were there it was a good night for them to try their hand at fortune telling because attempts at divination were thought to be particularly successful on that night.

When Christianity was introduced the date became the Eve of All Saints or All Hallows (November 1st), the word hallows being derived from the Old English word *halig*, holy. Some of the customs and beliefs of the Celtic festival were transferred to the Christian one and so retained their association with October 31st.

Old Customs

Anyone who is particularly interested in the old Halloween

customs and beliefs should read the poem *Halloween* by Robert Burns (*see* **Appendix**), although they will have to be prepared to try to understand the Scots language in which it is written. Many of these beliefs and customs were connected with the supernatural and the foretelling of the future. Evil spirits, often in the form of witches and warlocks, were still thought to roam the land and ghosts were also thought to put in regular appearances.

Romance and Marriage

Various acts of fortune telling were popular and often these related to romance and marriage. For example, two young people who were engaged or going out together would each put a nut on a fire. If the nuts burned without making much noise the future marriage of the couple would be a happy one. However, if the nuts burned noisily with sparks flying, any future alliance between the couple would be a stormy one. This same kind of information could be obtained also by burning two straws upright in the remains of a fire.

A young woman who wanted to know the identity or appearance of the person whom she would marry would reach for an apple, apples being long associated with Halloween. She would then eat it in front of a mirror, hoping that the face of her future husband would appear.

In order to discover how many children they were likely to have, young women would collect stalks of oat and count the seeds. Each seed represented a child.

If young people wanted to know the likely stature of their future spouses they would make their way to a field of kail (cabbage). There, having been blindfolded, they would pull stalks of kail. The physical shape of the kail would give an indication of that of their future spouse. Obviously, most people hoped for a long, slender, well-shaped stalk – and spouse.

Customs that have survived

The festival of Halloween is still celebrated in Scotland, although mostly it is now a festival for children. Some of the old customs and beliefs have had a marked effect on how the children celebrate.

The belief in witches, warlocks and ghosts has waned considerably across the decades and centuries, although some children may still have nightmares about them. You may, however, still spot some supernatural beings wandering around on Halloween, but these are likely to be children in disguise. They are guisers.

Guising

Guising, which obviously has linguistic connections with disguise, is an important feature of Halloween. Children dress up, usually as some character traditionally associated with Halloween, such as a witch, a ghost or a witch's cat. They then go round the doors of the neighbourhood, performing a song, poem or dance and getting some kind of treat, either sweets, nuts, fruits or a small sum of money, in return.

Historically, guising was not restricted to children and it was not restricted to Halloween. Originally guisers were mainly adults and the practice of guising was common in festivals such as New Year, Twelfth Night and May Day. Guisers would go round the neighbourhood in disguise seeking gifts of food and drink.

In the early days of Halloween people

wore false faces to disguise themselves. These masks depicted the faces of a supernatural creature, such as a witch, perhaps in the hope that the people wearing them would be indistinguishable from the evil spirits who were roaming the country and so would not be attacked by the 'real' supernatural creatures.

Turnip Lanterns

Turnips have long been associated with Halloween, probably because it is a common winter crop in Scotland

and so is readily available. Until very recently, it was a universal custom in the country to make a lantern from a turnip at Halloween.

The inside of the turnip is scooped out, or rather gouged out, because this is no easy task, until just a thin layer remains. Then eyes, a mouth and a nose are carved out of the outer surface of the turnip to make as grotesque a face as you want. Then a candle is placed in the inside of the turnip and a string is attached to the top. Hey presto, a turnip lantern!

Children sometimes carry turnip lanterns around when they go guising, but people are more safety conscious than they once were and the turnip lantern is an obvious fire hazard. Nowadays, it is often thought safer to leave the turnip lanterns in the windows at home, but not too close to the curtains!

Dookin' for Apples

A traditional Halloween custom that is still popular today involves apples. You fill a large bowl with

water and place a number of apples
in it. Then each person who is
taking part takes a fork in their
mouth and tries to spear an apple
with it. Occasionally people try
to catch the apples with their teeth.
This game is known as dookin' for
apples, which is Scots for
ducking for apples.

Treacle scones

Another traditional Halloween custom
which is still practised today, but which

is not so popular as dookin' for apples, involves spreading scones with lots of treacle. Threads from a beam or line of rope then hang the scones and people try to take a bite from the scones, when they are swinging around. Often the hands of the players are tied behind their backs to make the task harder. The result is a lot of sticky faces!

Change

Everything is subject to change and Halloween is no exception. The custom lives on, but it has, in many ways, suffered a sea change.

Guising new style

Scottish children still go guising, but, in many parts of the country, it is not the custom it once was. Communities are not as stable as they once were. People come and go and the children going guising do not always know their neighbours. This, coupled with the fact that modern parents are much more protective of their children than parents of previous generations were, means that adults often accompany the traditional child guisers.

Often the adults are anxious to get the whole thing over so that they can go home to dinner after a hard day at work. Thus, the children have little time to offer more than a quick rendition of one verse of their chosen poem and it's off back into the four-by-four standing, engine still running, at the pavement. Furthermore, some of today's children, who have been taught that the only skills that matter are entrepreneurial, are likely to turn their noses up at offerings of sweets and nuts and think that the only gift worth having is one of money.

Trick or treat

Recently the customs of this traditional festival have come under threat from customs that are popular in the American equivalent. Instead of guising, American children indulge in a custom known as trick or treat.

They, too, dress up, often as a character associated with Halloween, such as a witch or ghost, and they, too, go round the houses of their neighbourhood hoping to receive gifts of sweets, nuts, money, etc. The difference is that American children do not offer to entertain the various householders that they visit. Instead, they deliver a threat, which varies in severity, to the effect that they will play a trick on the householders if not given some form of treat.

Recently, the practice of trick or treat has come to Britain, probably because it has gained publicity from various American films. It is now commonly practised in various parts of England, although Halloween was rarely practised there. Furthermore, trick or treat is also having an influence in Scotland. It has not taken over from the original tradition, but it is confusing the issue at the very least.

Pumpkin lanterns

Pumpkin lanterns are an essential part of

the trick or treat culture. A few decades ago it would have been impossible for pumpkins to become part of the Scottish Halloween because they would not have been readily available. Nowadays, thanks to the globalisation of the produce shelves in supermarkets, pumpkins are in copious supply in Scotland in October.

The pumpkin lantern is definitely taking over from the turnip lantern. This may not be the result of the triumph of trick or treat over Halloween. Indeed, it is more likely to be down to the fact that a pumpkin lantern is much easier to make than a turnip one. Scooping out a pumpkin lantern is child's play compared to gouging out a turnip. Yet, to veterans of Halloween like myself, the pumpkin lantern looks like an alien amidst the traditional Halloween scene.

Adults

Perhaps owing to the influence of American films and television, Halloween in Britain is becoming much more of an adult festival than it ever was before and adult Halloween parties are now much more common. Admittedly, they are still much more common in smart London circles than in Scotland, even in the cities, but it is an ongoing trend.

Of course, adults do not ask for treats at Halloween, at least not round the neighbourhood. They do, however, dress up, but there the resemblance with the traditional children's Halloween party ends. At least at the smarter parties, many of the costumes have little to do with the traditional characters of witches and ghosts. They are much more sophisticated and innovative and the wearers of them certainly do not dook for apples or try to eat swinging treacle-covered scones.

November 5

In the early years of the Halloween festival, fire was an essential part of the proceedings and many bonfires were lit. As time went on, the bonfire connection with Halloween was lost, but now it is back, but with a different origin.

Increasingly, the traditions connected

with Halloween are becoming confused with those connected with Guy Fawkes. In England children go round for some days, or weeks, before November 5th saying 'a penny for the guy', asking people for money to help them build an effigy of Guy Fawkes, called a guy, and to buy fireworks to light round the bonfire where the effigy will burn.

Why should these festivals become confused? The Guy Fawkes festival, over the decades, has been much more celebrated in Scotland than Halloween ever was in England. Scottish children have had the best of both worlds and the festivals are very close in time.

Furthermore, in recent years there has been an influx of people from England coming to live in Scotland and some confusion has occurred between the two festivals. Perhaps it is because the word guising is becoming confused with the word guy.

Then there is, undoubtedly, a commercial element. Every occasion on the calendar now is accompanied by the maximum amount of commercialisation and made to last for as long as possible. As we all know, the start of Christmas gets earlier and earlier, now probably late August at the latest!

Halloween and Guy Fawkes are obvious commercial targets, coming, as they do, so close together in the calendar. One easily slides in to the other with maximum profits for the suppliers of products associated with them. Thus, we have bonfires and fireworks from before Halloween until well after Guy Fawkes. No wonder there is confusion between the two festivals.

HOGMANAY

Many countries of the world celebrate the last day of the year, but no country celebrates it quite so whole-heartedly as Scotland. In recognition of its importance in our calendar, we have a special name for it. In England and other countries the end-of-year festival is referred as New Year's Eve, in America it is known simply as New Years (or New Year's), but in Scotland we call it Hogmanay.

Name and Origin

Mystery surrounds the origin of the word. Many suggestions have been made and there has been much dispute over them. The most generally accepted suggestion is that Hogmanay is French in origin, being derived from the old French word *aguillaneuf*. This was used to refer to presents given on the last day of the year and to the festival itself. The French words *l'an neuf* mean New Year.

The French connection seems plausible enough. Hogmanay, like the aforementioned French festival, used to be an occasion for the exchange of gifts, although now these gifts tend to be restricted to those given to the host of the party that you are attending.

Then there is the fact that there has long been a connection between France and Scotland, a connection strengthened by the strong links that existed between France and Mary, Queen of Scots, who lived in France as a child and who was briefly queen of France. The Scots/French connection was known as the Auld Alliance and led to the introduction of many French words into the Scots language.

Edinburgh party

Recently Hogmanay in Scotland has become associated with the huge street party that takes place in Edinburgh and which is transmitted by television to many parts of the world. The fame of this party has spread and visitors flock to it from across the world. Edinburgh is a relatively small city and the number of tickets issued for the party has to be restricted to avoid overcrowding and unfortunate accidents.

At the street party there is music, both

traditional and pop, general jollification and, of course, drinking. Hogmanay is a night when the native drink comes into its own. At other times of the year wine and beer are drunk, but on Hogmanay whisky is the drink of choice, being used for a seemingly endless series of toasts.

Customs

The Edinburgh party may be the public face of Hogmanay but, in many ways, it is not the real Hogmanay. Many of the revellers at the Edinburgh street party are visitors who have come to the city to savour the spirit of Hogmanay. Most of the citizens of Edinburgh and most of the rest of the inhabitants of Scotland prefer to celebrate Hogmanay with family and friends.

Some of them might go to a local central point, such as the town or village square, to drink a toast to the New Year as midnight strikes, perhaps. Many more, however, will have hurried home from wherever they happened to be, anxious to be home with their closest family before the 'bells', that is before midnight is sounded by local church bells, Big Ben on the TV, etc.

Greeting the New Year

When midnight has sounded the greeting of the New Year begins with a vengeance. Many whisky glasses are clinked and much hand shaking goes on between both friends and strangers. The greeting is usually 'a happy new year' or 'a good new year', but the Scots version 'a guid new year' is also quite common.

Unlike their French friends, the Scots do not, as a general rule, go in much for kissing the cheeks of strangers. Hogmanay is an exception, although, unlike the French, the kissing of cheeks is usually a man/woman thing. The average macho Scotsman still baulks at kissing another man on the cheek.

Singing

When Scots become sentimental, not

to mention drunk, as they certainly do at Hogmanay, they have a tendency to break into song. The song that traditionally accompanies Hogmanay is entitled appropriately *A Good New Year*, (*A Guid New Year* in Scots).

Scots tend to sing the first few lines of this with great gusto. Thus, they sing loudly and enthusiastically *'A guid New Year tae ane and a', An' mony may ye see.'* which translates as *'A good New Year to one and all, And many may you see.'* Some even manage to add *'An during a' the years tae be. O happy may ye be.'* which translates as *'And during all the years to come, O happy may you be.'* There are other verses but these are largely forgotten by the singers, or never known by them in the first place.

There is another song associated with Hogmanay and indeed with most Scottish occasions. Entitled *Auld Lang Syne*, it is usually sung at the end of events. At Hogmanay it is often sung to welcome in the New Year. *See* **Appendix**.

First-footing

After the midnight exchange of greetings, some family members stay on to welcome guests, although a few party-poopers might slink off to bed. The rest go out to visit other members of the family, neighbours and friends.

This Hogmanay visiting is known as first-footing, although only the first person to enter a house after midnight is technically known as the first-foot. Traditionally, there are certain ideal requirements for a first-foot to have.

First, the person should be male and dark-haired and, preferably, tall. Such a person is thought to bring exceptionally good luck to the house that he first-foots.

An even more important requirement for a first-footer is that he carries a gift. Householders may reluctantly accept a first-foot who does not fit the ideal physical characteristics, but they will be very uneasy indeed if the first person to enter their house in the New Year is empty-handed, for it is widely believed that such a person will bring bad luck.

Quick-thinking householders may well spot the absence of a gift from the hands of their first-foot and quickly hand him something to carry in. Alternatively, there are various traditional actions that are taken to avert the bad luck brought by an empty-handed first-foot. These include throwing some salt in the fire and burning a piece of straw up the chimney.

Traditional Gifts

In modern times, what the first-foot is carrying is often just a bottle of whisky. This bottle is rarely presented to the host as a gift. Usually, the first-foot simply pours the host a drink from the bottle, and the host reciprocates the favour.

According to tradition, the first-foot is expected to bring a piece of coal, supposedly to ensure that there will be warmth and a copious supply of fuel in the house all year. Some form of food, often now some shortbread, is also traditional, to ensure a steady supply of sustenance in the house throughout the coming year.

Hogmanay Food

As has been mentioned above, shortbread is popular as a gift at New Year and it is an essential part of any traditional Hogmanay party. Equally traditional, but now less common, is black bun, which consists of a pastry case surrounding an incredibly rich fruitcake mixture. This is not for those who worry about their weight. One slice has enough calories to last your body most of January!

You might think that haggis, being a traditional Scottish food, would play a significant part in the New Year festivities, but this is not usually the case. Instead, a particularly popular savoury dish at New Year is steak pie. Those who wish to line their stomachs with something substantial to offset the effects of all the alcohol they will drink later often consume a hearty portion of steak pie and mashed potatoes before the Hogmanay celebrations begin. Some party hosts serve steak pie in the course of the evening, but the dish is more commonly eaten as part of a family meal on New Year's Day.

Special Festivals

Various parts of Scotland retain their own special Hogmanay festivals. For example, at the village of Comrie, in Perthshire they have a ceremony known as the Flambeaux. The flambeaux, or torches, consist of small trees the ends of which are covered in a combustible material soaked in paraffin. These are lit at midnight on Hogmanay and carried through the village. Decorated floats are also part of the procession which finishes at the village square where the flambeaux are then thrown together to make a bonfire.

At Stonehaven, near Aberdeen, there is a ceremony involving swinging fireballs. Men and women march along behind the town's pipe band, whirling flaming fireballs on lengths of rope above their heads. It is as well not to get too near them, especially since some of them may already have been celebrating the New Year. The balls, incidentally, are made from well-packed combustible material, wrapped in sacking, and then bound in wire netting.

The changing scene of Hogmanay

Nothing stays the same and this is as true of Hogmanay as anything else. It is undeniable that the festival's traditions are not so widely celebrated in Scotland as they once were partly because of social change.

Communities are not so close-knit as they once were. In towns and cities there is a much larger turnover of residents than there was a few decades ago, partly because people tend to move around more in connection with their jobs and partly because they move up the property ladder. Perhaps because of this swift turnover people tend not to be as close to their neighbours as they once were. They are more reserved and often they do not get to know their neighbours well enough to engage in first-footing.

Often one's family and friends now live in other places or, at best, at the other side of the town or city where you live. Because Hogmanay is such an alcoholic festival, many people are reluctant to be abstemious enough to remain legally able to drive. At the same time, public transport is not readily available, which is perfectly understandable. Bus drivers and taxi drivers have a right to celebrate as well.

The result is that it is much easier to stay at home than visit family and friends and, if you do not know your neighbours very well, there is a temptation to slump in front of the ubiquitous television set instead of playing an active part in the Hogmanay festivities.

The number of people who come to live in Scotland from other countries has played its part in the decline of the traditional Hogmanay. Incomers, of whom many in Scotland are English, are not always anxious to embrace the local traditions and customs of the country they move to. There again, many communities are reluctant to accept strangers until they have lived in the community for decades. This is even truer when the incomers are holiday-home owners and so only part-time members of the community. The result of this is that the newcomers often do not get involved in the Hogmanay celebrations.

The decline in Scotland's New Year festivities, however, is only relative. Thankfully, Hogmanay is still alive and well in Scotland!

APPENDIX

A Guid New Year

To a Haggis By Robert Burns

Fair fa' your honest, sonsie face,
Great chieftain o' the pudding-race!
Aboon them a' ye tak your place,
Painch, tripe, or thairm:
Weel are ye wordy o' a grace
As lang's my arm.

The groaning trencher there ye fill,

Your hurdies like a distant hill,
Your pin wad help to mend a mill
In time o' need,
While thro' your pores the dews distil
Like amber bead.

His knife see rustic Labour dight,
An' cut you up wi' ready sleight,
Trenching your gushing entrails bright,
Like ony ditch;
And then, O what a glorious sight,
Warm-reekin', rich!

Then, horn for horn, they
stretch an' strive:

Deil tak the hindmost! on they drive,
Till a' their weel-swall'd kytes belyve
Are bent like drums;
Then auld Guidman, maist like to rive,
Bethankit! hums.

Is there that owre his French ragout
Or olio that wad staw a sow,
Or fricassee wad make her spew
Wi' perfect sconner,
Looks down wi' sneering, scornfu' view
On sic a dinner?

Poor devil! see him owre his trash,
As feckles as wither'd rash,

His spindle shank, a guid whip-lash;
His nieve a nit;
Thro' bloody flood or field to dash,
O how unfit!

But mark the Rustic, haggis-fed,
The trembling earth resounds his tread.
Clap in his walie nieve a blade,
He'll mak it whissle;
An' legs an' arms, an' hands will sned,
Like taps o' thrissle.

Ye Pow'rs, wha mak mankind your care,
And dish them out their bill o' fare,

Auld Scotland wants nae skinking ware
That jaups in luggies;
But, if ye wish her gratefu' prayer
Gie her a haggis!

Halloween by Robert Burns

Yes! let the rich deride,
the proud disdain,
The simple pleasure of the lowly train;
To me more dear, congenial to my heart,
One native charm, than all the
gloss of art.–Goldsmith.

Upon that night, when fairies light
On Cassilis Downans dance,
Or owre the lays, in splendid blaze,
On sprightly coursers prance;
Or for Colean the rout is ta'en,
Beneath the moon's pale beams;
There, up the Cove, to stray an' rove,
Amang the rocks and streams
To sport that night;

Amang the bonie winding banks,
Where Doon rins, wimplin, clear;
Where Bruce ance rul'd the martial ranks,
An' shook his Carrick spear;

Some merry, friendly, countra-folks
Together did convene,
To burn their nits, an' pou their stocks,
An' haud their Halloween
Fu' blythe that night.

The lasses feat, an' cleanly neat,
Mair braw than when they're fine;
Their faces blythe, fu' sweetly kythe,
Hearts leal, an' warm, an' kin':
The lads sae trig, wi' wooer-babs
Weel-knotted on their garten;
Some unco blate, an' some wi' gabs
Gar lasses' hearts gang startin
Whiles fast at night.

Then, first an' foremost, thro' the kail,
Their stocks maun a' be sought ance;
They steek their een, and
grape an' wale
For muckle anes, an' straught anes.
Poor hav'rel Will fell aff the drift,
An' wandered thro' the bow-kail,
An' pou't for want o' better shift
A runt was like a sow-tail
Sae bow't that night.

Then, straught or crooked, yird or nane,
They roar an' cry a' throu'ther;
The vera wee-things, toddlin, rin,
Wi' stocks out owre their shouther:

An' gif the custock's sweet or sour,
Wi' joctelegs they taste them;
Syne coziely, aboon the door,
Wi' cannie care, they've plac'd them
To lie that night.

The lassies staw frae 'mang them a',
To pou their stalks o' corn;
But Rab slips out, an' jinks about,
Behint the muckle thorn:
He grippit Nelly hard and fast:
Loud skirl'd a' the lasses;
But her tap-pickle maist was lost,
Whan kiutlin in the fause-house
Wi' him that night.

*The auld guid-wife's weel-hoordit nits
Are round an' round dividend,
An' mony lads an' lasses' fates
Are there that night decided:
Some kindle couthie side by side,
And burn thegither trimly;
Some start awa wi' saucy pride,
An' jump out owre the chimlie
Fu' high that night.*

*Jean slips in twa, wi' tentie e'e;
Wha 'twas, she wadna tell;
But this is Jock, an' this is me,
She says in to hersel':
He bleez'd owre her, an' she owre him,*

As they wad never mair part:
Till fuff! he started up the lum,
An' Jean had e'en a sair heart
To see't that night.

Poor Willie, wi' his bow-kail runt,
Was brunt wi' primsie Mallie;
An' Mary, nae doubt, took the drunt,
To be compar'd to Willie:
Mall's nit lap out, wi' pridefu' fling,
An' her ain fit, it brunt it;
While Willie lap, and swore by jing,
'Twas just the way he wanted
To be that night.

Nell had the fause-house in her min',
She pits hersel an' Rob in;
In loving bleeze they sweetly join,
Till white in ase they're sobbin:
Nell's heart was dancin at the view;
She whisper'd Rob to leuk for't:
Rob, stownlins, prie'd her bonie mou',
Fu' cozie in the neuk for't,
Unseen that night.

But Merran sat behint their backs,
Her thoughts on Andrew Bell:
She lea'es them gashin at their cracks,
An' slips out-by hersel';
She thro' the yard the nearest taks,

*An' for the kiln she goes then,
An' darklins grapit for the bauks,
And in the blue-clue throws then,
Right fear't that night.*

*An' ay she win't, an' ay she swat—
I wat she made nae jaukin;
Till something held within the pat,
Good Lord! but she was quaukin!
But whether 'twas the deil himsel,
Or whether 'twas a bauk-en',
Or whether it was Andrew Bell,
She did na wait on talkin
To spier that night.*

Wee Jenny to her graunie says,
"Will ye go wi' me, graunie?
I'll eat the apple at the glass,
I gat frae uncle Johnie:"
She fuff't her pipe wi' sic a lunt,
In wrath she was sae vap'rin,
She notic't na an aizle brunt
Her braw, new, worset apron
Out thro' that night.

"Ye little skelpie-limmer's face!
I daur you try sic sportin,
As seek the foul thief ony place,
For him to spae your fortune:
Nae doubt but ye may get a sight!

Great cause ye hae to fear it;
For mony a ane has gotten a fright,
An' liv'd an' died deleerit,
On sic a night.

"Ae hairst afore the Sherra-moor,
I mind't as weel's yestreen-
I was a gilpey then, I'm sure
I was na past fyfteen:
The simmer had been cauld an' wat,
An' stuff was unco green;
An' eye a rantin kirn we gat,
An' just on Halloween
It fell that night.

"Our stibble-rig was Rab M'Graen,
A clever, sturdy fallow;
His sin gat Eppie Sim wi' wean,
That lived in Achmacalla:
He gat hemp-seed, I mind it weel,
An' he made unco light o't;
But mony a day was by himsel',
He was sae sairly frighted
That vera night."

Then up gat fechtin Jamie Fleck,
An' he swoor by his conscience,
That he could saw hemp-seed a peck;
For it was a' but nonsense:
The auld guidman raught

down the pock,
An' out a handfu' gied him;
Syne bad him slip frae' mang the folk,
Sometime when nae ane see'd him,
An' try't that night.

He marches thro' amang the stacks,
Tho' he was something sturtin;
The graip he for a harrow taks,
An' haurls at his curpin:
And ev'ry now an' then, he says,
"Hemp-seed I saw thee,
An' her that is to be my lass
Come after me, an' draw thee
As fast this night."

*He wistl'd up Lord Lennox' March
To keep his courage cherry;
Altho' his hair began to arch,
He was sae fley'd an' eerie:
Till presently he hears a squeak,
An' then a grane an' gruntle;
He by his shouther gae a keek,
An' tumbled wi' a wintle
Out-owre that night.*

*He roar'd a horrid murder-shout,
In dreadfu' desperation!
An' young an' auld come rinnin out,
An' hear the sad narration:
He swoor 'twas hilchin Jean M'Craw,*

Or crouchie Merran Humphie-
Till stop! she trotted thro' them a';
And wha was it but grumphie
Asteer that night!

Meg fain wad to the barn gaen,
To winn three wechts o' naething;
But for to meet the deil her lane,
She pat but little faith in:
She gies the herd a pickle nits,
An' twa red cheekit apples,
To watch, while for the barn she sets,
In hopes to see Tam Kipples
That vera night.

She turns the key wi' cannie thraw,
An' owre the threshold ventures;
But first on Sawnie gies a ca',
Syne baudly in she enters:
A ratton rattl'd up the wa',
An' she cry'd Lord preserve her!
An' ran thro' midden-hole an' a',
An' pray'd wi' zeal and fervour,
Fu' fast that night.

They hoy't out Will, wi' sair advice;
They hecht him some fine braw ane;
It chanc'd the stack he faddom't thrice
Was timmer-propt for thrawin:
He taks a swirlie auld moss-oak

For some black, grousome carlin;
An' loot a winze, an' drew a stroke,
Till skin in blypes cam haurlin
Aff's nieves that night.

A wanton widow Leezie was,
As cantie as a kittlen;
But och! that night, amang the shaws,
She gat a fearfu' settlin!
She thro' the whins, an' by the cairn,
An' owre the hill gaed scrievin;
Whare three lairds' lan's met at a burn,
To dip her left sark-sleeve in,
Was bent that night.

Whiles owre a linn the burnie plays,
As thro' the glen it wimpl't;
Whiles round a rocky scar it strays,
Whiles in a wiel it dimpl't;
Whiles glitter'd to the nightly rays,
Wi' bickerin', dancin' dazzle;
Whiles cookit undeneath the braes,
Below the spreading hazel
Unseen that night.

Amang the brachens, on the brae,
Between her an' the moon,
The deil, or else an outler quey,
Gat up an' ga'e a croon:
Poor Leezie's heart maist lap the hool;

Near lav'rock-height she jumpit,
But mist a fit, an' in the pool
Out-owre the lugs she plumpit,
Wi' a plunge that night.

In order, on the clean hearth-stane,
The luggies three are ranged;
An' ev'ry time great care is ta'en
To see them duly changed:
Auld uncle John, wha wedlock's joys
Sin' Mar's-year did desire,
Because he gat the toom dish thrice,
He heav'd them on the fire
In wrath that night.

Wi' merry sangs, an' friendly cracks,
I wat they did na weary;
And unco tales, an' funnie jokes–
Their sports were cheap an' cheery:
Till butter'd sowens, wi' fragrant lunt,
Set a' their gabs a-steerin;
Syne, wi' a social glass o' strunt,
They parted aff careerin
Fu' blythe that night.

Auld Lang Syne By Robert Burns

Should auld acquaintance be forgot,
And never brought to mind?
Should auld acquaintance be forgot,
And auld lang syne!

Chorus:

For auld lang syne, my dear,

For auld lang syne.
We'll tak a cup o' kindness yet,
For auld lang syne.

And surely ye'll be your pint stowp!
And surely I'll be mine!
And we'll tak a cup o' kindness yet,
For auld lang syne.

Chorus

We twa hae run about the braes,
And pou'd the gowans fine;
But we've wander'd mony a weary fit,
Sin' auld lang syne.

Chorus

We twa hae paidl'd in the burn,
Frae morning sun till dine;
But seas between us braid hae roar'd
Sin' auld lang syne.

Chorus

And there's a hand, my trusty fiere!
And gie's a hand o' thine!
And we'll tak a right
gude-willie waught,
For auld lang syne.

Chorus

OTHER SCOTTISH FESTIVALS

There are so many Scottish festivals and celebrations that they cannot all be noted in such a small book as this.

This section deals with some of the

more popular and well-known festivals.

Without any bias, it makes sense to look at some of the more prominent, summer festivals in Edinburgh: the capital's festivals are now of substantial economic gain to the city and to Scotland in general. The impact of the summer festivals in Edinburgh alone is assessed on a rolling basis. Recent reports suggest that the city's summer festivals alone generate an extraordinary expenditure of some £130m in capital, and sustain the equivalent of 2,500-3,000 jobs across the country.

January

Burning the Clavie

Following an old tradition in Burghead, Morayshire, every year on the 11th of January, a tar barrel (which has been filled with wood shavings soaked in tar) is taken around the harbour and then on to the Doorie Hill where it is said the Celtic Druids used to light their fires.

Up Helly-aa

This festival is held in Lerwick, the Shetland Islands, on the last Tuesday of January. A full-scale Viking galley, complete with shields and oars, is pulled down to the beach by a torch-bearing group of people dressed as Viking warriors, no less! Three cheers for the builders of the narrow wooden ship are followed by a bugle call, then the galley is set alight by 800 burning torches.

Also in January:

1st: New Year Day (first footing)
1st: New Year Ba' Game,
   Kirkwall, Orkney
6th: Uphaillie Day

12th: Old New Year's Day
25th: Burns' Night

FEBRUARY

2nd: Candlemas Day
14th: St Valentine's Day

MARCH

Whuppity Scoorie

On the first day of March the boys of Lanark take part in a noisy, exuberant celebration; a legacy of the days when making a big racket was thought to scare off the evil spirits. Traditionally, pennies supplied by the Common Good Fund were hurled and the children would scramble to pick them up.

Also in March:
25th: Original New Year

APRIL

Hunt the Gowk

Known today in Britain as April Fools' Day, the 1st of April is of course when people have until noon to play tricks and tell fibs to catch each other out.

In Scotland this day was originally referred to as Huntigowk (or Hunt the Gowk Day), when the aim was to send someone on a foolish errand:

*Dinna laugh, an' dinna smile
But hunt the gowk another mile.*

Also in April:
2nd: Preen-tail Day or Tailie Day

MAY

1st: Beltane's Day
1st: May Day
1st: Robin Hood Games

24th: Victoria Day
24th: Empire Day

JUNE

Guid Nychburris

This is a Dumfries-based festival that takes place in mid June. It has its origins in a court established to resolve disputes between local people to make them 'guid nychburris' (good neighbours).

Lanimer Day

Held in Lanark, on the 17th of June,

Lanimer (merely an altered form of the word 'landmark' or boundary) Day is when people decorate their houses with green foliage and the Lanimer Fair takes place.

Selkirk Common Riding

This is a traditional ceremony known as Riding the Marches (or boundaries) and takes place on the 18th of June in Selkirk, where the Battle of Flodden (June, 1488) is commemorated. There are similar festivities to the Selkirk event which take place on differing dates in places such as Annan, Linlithgow and Peebles.

Also in June:
21st: Midsummer's Eve
24th: St John's Eve
25th: Whitsun
29th: Petermas

JULY

Glasgow Fair

The Glasgow Fair was established in 1190 by a charter from William I of Scotland ('The Lion'). It was originally a fair for selling horses and cattle etc.

but over time gradually evolved; by the 19th century it included theatres and circuses. From the early 1800s the event was held on the Green, near the River Clyde. By Victorian times the fair was the main summer holiday event for the people of the city. The fair takes place during the last two weeks of July.

AUGUST

Edinburgh International Festival

The Edinburgh International Festival is a major event in the late summer that offers visitors the chance to see performances of classical music, opera, theatre, dance, and comedy in an assortment of venues in the city. The Festival is a registered charity and, apart from the popular summer events, has a less well-known year-round programme of education work aimed at all ages.

The Festival is now famous across the world and attracts, quite rightly, a staggering amount of visitors each year. According to statistics for the 2004 Festival, about 60% of the audience came from Scotland, a quarter from the rest of the UK and the remainder from overseas.

The principal venues used are as follows (with the figure in brackets indicating the capacity for each venue):

The Edinburgh Playhouse (2,900)
The Festival Theatre (1,800)
The Hub (420)
The King's Theatre (1,300)
The Queen's Hall (920)
The Royal Lyceum Theatre (650)
The Usher Hall (2,300).

These venues aside, there is plenty of free street theatre adding to the festivities.

Edinburgh Fringe Festival

The Fringe Festival began life in a disused pub with a dodgy roof near the Royal Mile but its days of being seen as the poor cousin of the Edinburgh International Festival are over.

The Fringe's founding aim was to provide open-access for all performers and it has grown in popularity ever since, with over a million tickets (worth more than £10m in total) being sold each year.

Edinburgh International Book Festival

The Edinburgh International Book Festival is the world's biggest book festival.

It has a wide-ranging programme for adults and children alike, including discussions, author readings, lectures, debates and short courses, all in Charlotte Square Gardens.

Edinburgh International Film Festival

The first Edinburgh International Film Festival took place in 1947 and is now the longest continually running film festival in the world

Originally a documentary-based event, established after WWII, the early years of the Festival saw premieres of classics such as Robert Flaherty's Louisiana Story and Roberto Rossellini's Germany Year. Since then it has paid tribute to the diverse talents of the likes of Sam Fuller, John Huston, and a young Martin Scorsese. Notable screenings of the last few years have included: The Full Monty, East is East, Billy Elliot, Amélie, Motorcycle Diaries, and La Vie Revée des Anges.

The Edinburgh Military Tattoo

The first Edinburgh Tattoo was staged in 1950 and is now a well-established Scottish tradition; the average annual Tattoo audience reaching around 217,000, with some 100 million people watching it each year on television around the world. At the last official independent count, visitors to the Tattoo contributed an estimated £88m to the Scottish economy.

Indeed, the Tattoo has a proud history of no performance ever having been cancelled. According to official reports, the 2005 Tattoo was the seventh successive sell-out season, generating some £3.9 million in box office receipts. Set up and run for charitable purposes, over the years The Tattoo has given some £5m to service and civilian organisations.

The Tattoo has always been staged at Edinburgh Castle. The 1000-

stronge cast of players rehearse at Redford Barracks, Edinburgh.

The word 'tattoo' comes from the closing-time cry in the inns in the Low Countries during the 17th and 18th centuries - 'Doe den tap toe' ('Turn off the taps').

Also in August:
1st: Lammas
15th: Marymas

SEPTEMBER

The Braemar Gathering

This Highland Games event takes place on the first Saturday in September and has quite a royal connection: its origins can be traced back to the 11th century when King Malcolm III of Scotland presented a prize to the winner of a race to the top of Craig Choinnich. Queen Victoria attended the Gathering in 1848 and the Royal family has been associated with the event ever since.

Also in September:

27th: Feast of St Barr

28th: Michaelmas Eve

29th: Michaelmas Day

OCTOBER

St Luke's Day

The 18th of October is also known as Sour Cakes Day in Scotland. This goes back to particular celebrations in the Royal Burgh of Rutherglen, and the baking of cakes eaten with sour cream.

NOVEMBER

1st: All Saints Day
5th: Bonfire Night / Guy Fawkes
11th: Martinmas
30th: St Andrew's Day

DECEMBER

6th: St Nicholas Eve
21st: St Thomas Day
21st: Barring-out Day
24th: Christmas Eve
25th: Christmas Day
26th: Sweetie Scone Day

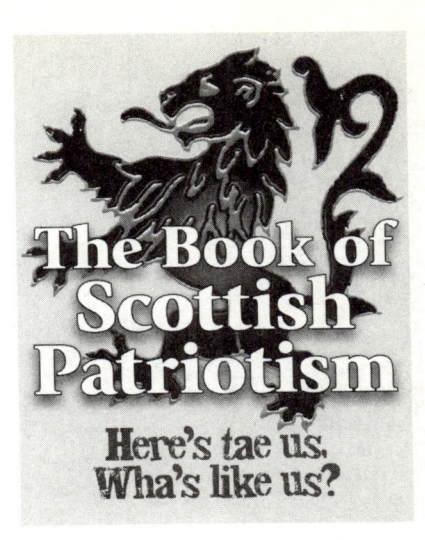

The Book of Scottish Patriotism
1-905102-29-1, £4.99

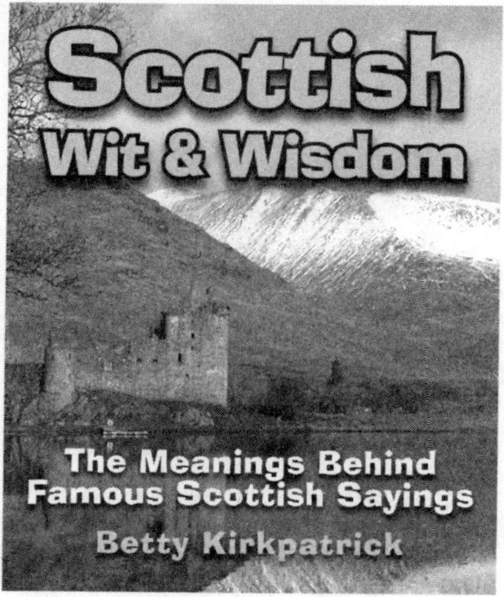

Scottish Wit & Wisdom
1-905102-07-0, £2.99

124

Auld Scottish Grannies' Remedies
1-905102-06-2, £2.99

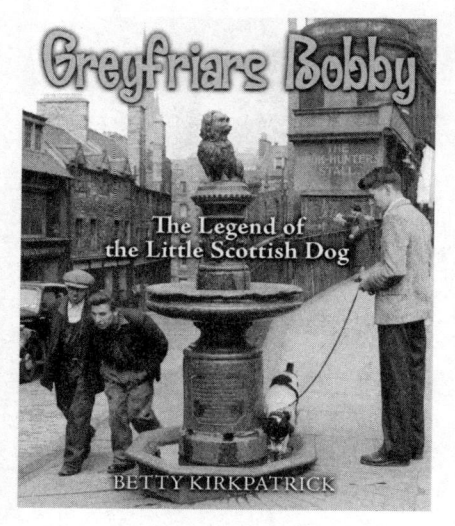

Greyfriars Bobby
1-905102-04-6, £2.99

Nessie

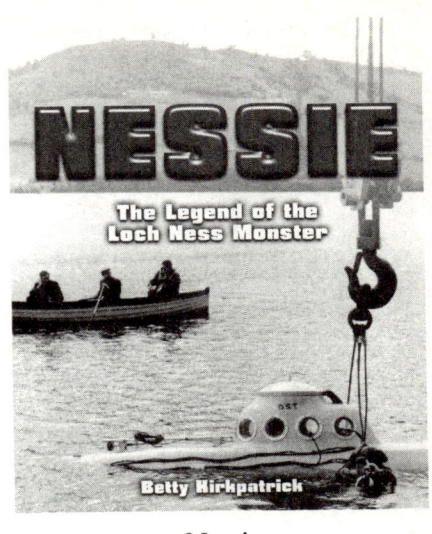

1-905102-05-4, £2.99

For more Scottish-interest
titles, please visit

www.crombiejardine.com/scots